GW00597356

LCS.

LifeCoach School international

Personal Performance Coaching A-Z

7 days to a New You!

Compiled by PaTrisha Anne Todd

Published in the United Kingdom by Picerjaw & Co Ltd
Bournemouth, Dorset, England

www.picerjaw.com

The moral right of each of the authors is hereby asserted.

A catalogue record for this book is available from the British Library.

ISBN 0-9543262-2-9
Self help/Inspirational

£12.99

Cover and Inside Design by:
Kathryn Patrick

Technical Consultation:
Benjamin Wilfred

Further Consultation:
W Todd

Editing team at LCSi - LifeCoach School international.

Set in Palatino Linotype
Point 12

Dedication

This book is dedicated to all my coaching clients – current, past and future. Each of you have in your unique way allowed me to work with you in partnership towards your own goals both personal and business, thus letting me share the journey of those goals as you realise each of your triumphs.

I also give thanks to my mother, father and my children who have throughout the years inspired and fueled by beliefs and helped me to turn my dreams into reality.

God bless you all.

List of Contents

The mini-course - *7 Days to a New You!*

LCSi - LifeCoach School international

presents

Personal Performance Coaching is the approaching of your spirit to visit your required...

From my private collection written for me...

A   achievement potential, to remove the

B   blockage, which is essential, to

C   culminate and so celebrate, the

D   deliverance of your depression and release the...

E   energy of your inspiration, so to

F   forge ahead and have spiritual faith, in your Self-

G   guidance to generate your,

H   higher self and to heal your fright, so to,

I   inspire your inner-sight, to,

J   journey with jubilation, to your Self-

K   knowledge and kindness, your,

L   love of live, to lift your blindness, and gain,

M   mental spiritual initiative, to remove the

N   no, no and the negative, so to,

O   open your self-opinion for opportunity, to

P   positive power and prosperity, towards,

Q   quality of life and quintessence, of your,

R   right to re-al-ise the reality of your inner presence, your,

S   strength and true spirit,

T   to remove your taboo and let your teleology visit, just,

Y   you, just you, only you,

V   vacate your negative for victory and remove,

W   weakness and welcome wholesomeness,

INTRODUCTION

Wow, what has life given you up until now?

I was speaking with one of my closest friends while we were on the other side of the planet far away from good old UK. We were in Surfers Paradise, Australia. We were just two busy people taking time out, looking at other busy people watching them, watching us, watching them. We were doing all of this while raising our consciousness on the topic of life and achieving the optimum personal performance.

Our surroundings were simply lush and we were surrounded by high value net worth individuals all motivated individuals who regularly and consciously step out of their comfort zone (The Circle of Life), to achieve the life they truly desire and deserve.

No one man or woman is born without a desire to succeed in his or her own life. The trouble is with 90% of the population is that they choose to stay where they are. While the other 10% have a hunger to achieve more, and an amazing 3% in that group are the real movers and shakes of this place. My personal goal is to become one of those 3% statistics, and to go down in history as a business woman of inspiration sharing my passion and core values that I hold close to my heart. They are my family, spirituality, integrity, creating high value experiences for my clients, profitability and helping those who need charity to begin the process of their empowerment.

As part of that goal I have created *'Personal Performance Coaching A-Z'*.
It's a book offering the reader tools towards a sense of mind, body and spirit, giving the reader an opportunity to build self belief, confidence and blow out self-sabotage. The book is a real personal relationship with oneself and with others. The pages offer insights into creating a lifestyle that holds happiness, health and success. The bonus is that at the back of the book you will find the section on *'7 days to a new you'* a mini self coaching course. Take a look.

The case studies are the stories of those determined individuals who have studied hard to achieve their graduation from LCSi as professional Personal Performance Coaches. It is they who have contributed to the book.

Amazingly through the documentation of others personal journey an example is demonstrated into how one can move from a place of challenge to a place of satisfying living. Each story reflects a different level of living. It is hoped that you enjoy the words and draw inspiration to *Live Your Life by Design*.

A great number of beliefs are born from an unknown source. That source can be the idea of others who traditionally accept the thoughts and ideas of others and of the Great Architect of the Universe. But, you know what, a strong core belief and faith can transform yesterdays' impossibilities into today's possibilities. I hope that as you read this book you will be inspired to transform you lifestyle for the better.

These stories are not about any one person, rather they are experiences and thoughts of others who have released their limiting beliefs and stepped out of their comfort zone to turn their lifestyle around. They have accessed their *infinite intelligence*, the source of wisdom and thought power. However, you need to be totally committed to changing your life from the inside out and go that extra mile. You can do that by re-programming your subconscious mind to be predominantly positive with predetermined life goal. You have to choose to live your life on purpose. I'll help you to do that, if you like.

To the
Ambassador's of
Personal Performance Coaching A-Z

my heartfelt thanks for your support in making this book happen!

Joy Allen

Halley Brentt

Claire Conroy

John Ellis

Ann Fieldhouse

Margaret Haffenden

Rose Hebbron

Marusja Harasymiw

Francelyn Lewis

Anthony Matthews

Simran Ranu

PaTrisha-Anne Todd

A selection of personal performance coaching
case studies by
LCSi - LifeCoach School international
graduate students from around the world.

Read each story and enjoy the message the
Ambassadors offer you.

Contact them via

Find A Coach @ www.lcsi.co.uk

A contribution by

Joy Allen

A graduate LCSi - LifeCoach School international student from England.

THE JOY OF TRANSFORMATION

Transformation can come into our life in many different ways, sometimes through choice sometimes through unforeseen circumstances, whichever way it happens we all need guidance and support to help us on this part of our journey through life.

This support can come from friends, family or a professional person, but mostly it's about having a positive mental attitude and making a commitment to yourself to attain your goal.

There are many reasons and circumstances that force us to make some changes either, emotional, work related, relationships, financial, unhappiness or dissatisfaction with life in general, and if we don't see the signs and address the imbalance in our life this can manifest as illness.

This is what happened to me, I valued material things more than I valued myself. I was working twelve hour days, feeling stressed, not eating properly, spreading myself to thinly, not taking time out to rest and nurture myself and this all contributed to being diagnosed in 1999 with breast cancer. I didn't see the signs, I depleted my immune system until it couldn't cope anymore, I was facing a huge STOP sign in my life and was being forced to look at myself and the way I was living my life. The diagnosis wasn't good, as the cancer had spread to my lymph glands these were removed whilst also having a mastectomy, this was followed by ten months of chemotherapy and five weeks of radiotherapy, but I was very fortunate to be introduced to a holistic charity called "New Approaches to Cancer", and with there support and guidance, combining the holistic along with conventional medicine I came through my journey through cancer and made a good recovery.

It was while I was recovering that I took a good long look at my life and reassessed my priorities, I realised that all my life I had been looking at all the externals in life thinking these would make me happy and they hadn't, I had kept on searching for the next thing to make me feel happy to give me that inner contentment and suddenly I had it. I realised for the first time how loved I was by others and this had filtered through to me and I started to love and accept myself. I'd taken things for granted, my health especially, I hadn't known it was the little things in life that are important, being there for someone, giving up your time, sharing special times and accepting people as they are, we are all unique. The gifts I received on my healing journey through cancer are Gratitude for each day, Tolerance for myself and others, Faith and Trust in the universe, and Learning to love myself as I am.

So to complete my transformation I returned to work on a part time basis, and I made a decision to live a more balanced life, taking time out to nurture and respect myself and put boundaries in place by planning in time for myself instead of everyone else. I was training to be a Psychosynthesis counsellor and whilst I felt I could help others on their path, it didn't feel the right path for me. I believe that people come into your life for a reason and It was then that I was guided towards PaTrisha-Anne at the Life Coach School international where I found that I could train to be a Holistic Coach, this was exactly what I was looking for and with PaTrisha-Anne's guidance I completed my training and set up my own practice, calling it "The Joy of Transformation," as I feel this says it all, as it is not only my name but my own experience of transformation and how I can help others make the changes they desire in there life.

I am now a qualified Holistic Coach working with the Mind, Body and Spirit, giving guidance and support to clients helping them to make those changes and bring balance and harmony into their life which enables them to move forwards and achieve their goal. I also work alongside the holistic charity that gave support to me. I have set up weekly Self Development classes using the Circle of Life, a coaching tool that helps us to look at the balance of our life as it is at this moment in time. The Circle of Life is divided into eight sections each representing an area of our life; the sections are Home & Family, Finance/Wealth, Work/business, Friends, Spirituality, Health/nutrition, Fun activities/ leisure and Partnerships.

The centre of the circle represents least satisfied with at the moment and the score is 0, the outer circle represents the most satisfied with right now and score 10. Each week we take a section of the circle and look at this area in detail, measuring our level of satisfaction between 0 and 10, we then look at ways we can improve upon this and each person agrees a task to action by the following week, they are making this commitment to themselves to help them move forward. Over the eight weeks a picture is building up of how the balance of there life is at this moment and any areas that may need extra attention on their healing journey, its all very gentle and about self empowerment to move forward, it may only be baby steps but it is the first step on their journey towards balance and harmony.

I have also set up relaxation classes, with guided visualisation and meditation, this is about learning some relaxation techniques that can be done at home and also how to work with the Chakras, these are the energy centres through which we receive, transmit and process life energies, they are the network through which body, mind and spirit interact as one holistic system, they are openings through which our attitudes and belief systems enter in and create our body/mind structure, the energy created from our emotions and mental attitude, runs through the Chakras and this is distributed to our cells, tissues and organs. This realisation can bring tremendous insight into how we affect our bodies, minds and circumstances, and as we understand the Chakras we begin to understand ourselves and can make choices and decisions from a place of awareness and balance.

As well as running classes, I give talks to groups and run workshops on how we can through taking a Holistic approach to our life gain self empowerment to make the right choices for ourselves.

Joys story "MY GIFT OF CANCER". can be read on the New Approaches website   www.anac.org.uk   or   email   joy.allen3@btinternet.com

EMERGE TO YOUR FULL POTENTIAL & ACHIEVE YOUR DREAMS

JOY ALLEN- Holistic coach – Spiritual Journey Practitioner [SJP, LCSi]

Our inner self creates our outer reality and when we have an awareness of how the Mind, Body and Spirit work together to bring balance and harmony into our life, we begin to understand ourselves, and we can then from a place of self-empowerment change our lives.

As a Holistic Coach I give guidance and support to you on your journey to attain your goal, this can be by telephone, or face to face, all I ask is that you give 100% commitment to yourself, in this way you will achieve your dreams.

Email   joy.allen3@btinternet.com

Telephone 0208 751 3173

A contribution by

Halley Brentt

A graduate LCSi – LifeCoach School international student from Canada.

COMET COACHING

This collection of statements and phrases are both new and old. In the same way the different religions of earth all reflect and evolve around one Source and Creator. The following phrases of A – Z wordings speak of a universal truth in the language and specific depth that reflects the core rhythm that pulsates the heart of COMET COACHING...

To be consciously AWARE is key in all situations.

BEAUTY is in the eye of the beholder.

The only thing constant is CHANGE.

No two people will have the same diet, as we all digest like differently. Just like an onion with many layers of skin, we are manifested and enlightened at specific DEPTHS of being.

Everything is ENERGY at a different vibration.

We are different FREQUENCIES of the same Source.

Free yourself from emotional attitudes by carrying only an attitude of GRATTITUDE.

Believer in the three H's of HAPPY, HEALTHY, HOLY living.

One's INTUITION and IMAGINATION are very important. Especially for those interested in moving to the next dimension.

Life is a JOKE, it is not as serious as we believe it to be. Along with the great mysteries and wonders here on earth, there is much humour. Especially in us humans, so laugh; as " He who laughs...lasts."

KEEP up with evolution, the universe is constantly evolving, are you?

LOVE is the answer to every question....so.....serve with LOVE.

Life is MOVEMENT on physical, mental, and spiritual planes. Therefore when there is no MOVEMENT on these planes, death starts creeping in.

Step into the power of NOW. There will never be a better moment for you to shine.

...know in your soul, like your blood knows the way, from your heart to your brain, knows that your whOle...

PERSPECTIVE, use it or loose it.

QUALITY over quantity.

Learning is REMEMBERING.

We are SPIRITUAL beings on a human journey.

THRIVE to get exactly what you want in life, never settle for less than your hearts desire.

The UPWARD flow is a powerful vertical force connecting you to the Source. The trinity, the chakras and many other systems are born in this vortex.

To VALUE life as good or bad, right and wrong is so earthly, so human. Shift your language to a universal frequency where duality seizes, where things simply 'are', where there 'is', where "I AM"

How WONDERFUL to have been chosen to be 'here-now'

You may never receive an equal expression of the value of energy you e-XUDE. The secret is in the joy. Do it for the sheer joy of life, where your value is paid in the richness of passionate living.

The only thing that matters in YOU! Begin with yourself before being a martyr to the world.

ZIP to the next level in your life more shiftly by choosing to incorporate COMET COACHING into your life!

Halley Brentt, LCSi   "Coaching to higher dimensions"

www.halleybrentt.com

A contribution by

Claire Conroy

A graduate LCSi – LifeCoach School international
student from Ireland.

ARE YOU READY TO TAKET THIS CALL?

Pa Trisha-Anne's voice sounded crisp and fresh at 7.00 a.m. on the morning of January 16 2002 just over a year since the death of my husband and when I was still in a bad way emotionally because of the bereavement. PaTrisha-Anne was kind, compassionate and caring, yet she gently urged me to proceed with this course and so begin the process of my own coaching.

She encouraged me to take on small projects which would reclaim areas of my life which I could put my own stamp on. I chose to refurbish and redecorate my bedroom which had been *our* bedroom, but now I was reclaiming it as my own space - somewhere I could go and hide, or cry, or read or sleep as the mood was on me. Naturally I would crawl in there when I was emotionally low. This room became my sanctuary. PaTrisha-Anne also coached me on the craft of coaching and the process involved in becoming a Life Coach. Thus I was already on the path towards creating my new life.

liked it. The ceiling was white and the walls a pale pink colour, called 'Pastiche' so we only had to prepare the surfaces and apply a single coat of the same coloured paints. This was actually the first time I had ever used a roller as I had always used a paintbrush before when I had been decorating! One of my sons painted the skirting board and door frames. We did not bother painting the doors then as they had been painted only a year earlier.

Velazquez & Michelangelo

The weekend after the carpet was fitted we replaced the furniture - the bed, the bookcase and my lovely writing desk. I had bought a Victorian clock with a Roman clock face and lovely Victorian characters painted on the lacquered wooden surround. I had seen the clock in a shop in York on a family visit to my sister. I also had two prints which I framed and hung on the same wall as the clock, facing the bed. The first, from the Sistine Chapel, is of the Creation of Adam; the panel where the hand of God transforms the limp arm of Adam by giving him life. John and I had bought it on a trip to Rome on our 30th Wedding Anniversary. We had both been really impressed by the paintings on

Michelangelo's ceiling. In fact I am nuts about Michelangelo. The print we bought is also my favourite. The job of hanging all of these items up at just the right heights took a little measuring and a few mistakes but the final arrangement met with my artistic approval. The second print was a nude 'The Toilet of Venus' by Velazquez. This was a painting we had admired as students, when on a trip to London, and which John had bought a print of many years later. We had never actually displayed it then because we felt it might embarrass our sons some of whom were then already teenagers.

I had built the bedroom colour scheme around the two shades of dark wood in the room. One was the mahogany and the second was the lighter, more 'orangey', stained wood of the wardrobes. I integrated these two colours using a purple and orange striped duvet cover. The orange stripes were terra cotta really as were the curtains. The 'pastiche' walls were nearly the flesh tints used by Velazquez and Michelangelo. My sanctuary was taking shape. Next I cleaned the windows and washed and re-hung the terra cotta coloured curtains, I cleaned and really polished all of the furniture and carefully arranged my books in the bookcase.

The piece de resistance came in the form of a stool and the headboard. These were fabric covered pieces whose colour no longer suited the room. So I hunted for just the right shade and texture of fabric and had these re-covered. The whole process had taken months, with research and shopping trips interspersed with the other activities. By now I was sold on the definition of success as being the *journey* towards achieving a goal rather than just the *achievement* of the goal. This became meaningful activity. Of course I also celebrated the success of achieving it - of creating my sanctuary.

The Workbooks and Case Studies

By now I was working my way through the LCSi Workbooks. I found the concepts strange at first despite my achievement with the bedroom. Each time I came back to them, though, they made more sense. I had written to PaTrisha-Anne at one stage that it was a lot like learning a foreign language. It took a while for the vocabulary of Coaching to gel with me, particularly since many of the concepts came from NLP which I had not studied previously, but once they did come together I began to enjoy the many models, tools and strategies available.

When it came to case studies I remember one night phoning PaTrisha-Anne and saying 'Help! I've got a Client. What on earth am I going to say to her?' PaTrisha-Anne, of course, was not put out at all and proceeded to coach me on coaching my first client. Each Coach call was preceded by an almost panic on my part but I managed to get through them and I think I succeeded in helping those people to focus, to plan and to achieve their short term goals. I helped these clients to formulate and create plans for one long term, one medium term and one a short term goal. I even quoted PaTrisha-Anne's mantra that *'Coaching Leads To Success'*. I can say that coaching has become a lot got easier!

Many Projects

Since January 2002 I have refurbished and decorated my bedroom, landscaped the back garden, installed a new kitchen and central heating unit, dealt with leaking roofs over the study and the garden shed, travelled in Britain, Ireland, the US and France and decorated other bedrooms, one for the second time after a small fire!

I qualified as a Master Life and Business Coach and as a Master NLP Practitioner. Currently I am pursuing studies in Spirituality to become a Spiritual Journey Accompanier. Another branch of my Business involves teaching IT. During this time too I have passed my Driving Test, and have written a computer book which I use as teaching material for my students. I teach adult beginners how to use a computer and can bring them up to ECDL level using Microsoft Office.

Claire Conroy, LCSi   www.easysteps.org

A contribution by

John Ellis

A graduate LCSi – LifeCoach School international student from England.

FIVE TRAGEDIES TO TRIUMPH

I was born fifty years ago and lived my early childhood in a two-up, two down terraced house in the Manchester suburbs.

Very early on in my childhood I realised that I was from a very poor family compared to other kids. Normal meals consisted of bananas in milk, often toast and jam, and when my parents had virtually no money, just biscuits.

Clothes were second-hand. Jumble sales provided most of my clothing as they did my toys. My parents gave me plenty of love and spent whatever they could on me.

By the age of 12 I started to earn some money for myself babysitting for my Uncle and Auntie's daughter. My Uncle, who was only in his mid twenties had become incredibly rich in the space of just three years. He owned several sports cars, a string of shops, a car hire business and even his own small aircraft.

One night babysitting I was as bored as ever. There was nothing of interest on the television and I noticed a bookshelf full of books. I removed them one by one to glance through them and was fascinated by the titles. Books like "Think and Grow Rich", "How to Win Friends and Influence People" and others with various titles about becoming a millionaire.

On my babysitting nights I would spend hours reading the different chapters and at an early age I set my own goals of who I wanted to be and how I was going to do it.

My goal of becoming a fire fighter materialised as soon as I was 18. I left home and bought my own three bedroom semi-detached house – quite an achievement for someone so young in those days. I earned lots of extra money on top of my salary with lots of different business ideas. I painted houses, I cleaned windows

31

and I sold books by mail order. Life was great. By the age of 22 I was driving fast, expensive cars, had great holidays abroad and dressed in the latest fashionable clothes.

My first of many tragedies came one dark Sunday, wintry night. Whilst fighting a fire I became trapped in a building and could not escape. The last thing I remember was seeing my life quickly flash by as I gasped for breath in the toxic fumes from the fire. I woke up the next day in hospital – miraculously I had been rescued by other fire fighters who had put me, unconscious, into the back of an ambulance.

Physically and mentally I was too affected by my injuries to carry on and I retired from the Fire Service after just four years of fulfilling my dream career.

I joined a small company selling fire alarm systems. For five years I worked incredibly hard. Fifteen hour days were the norm. I applied all the lessons I had learnt in my Uncle's books. The company made hundreds of thousands of pounds of profits because of me. The owner was so pleased that he promised me a massive bonus on top of my alary. Of course that never materialised and then to my horror the owner sold the company to a competitor. He became an overnight millionaire and my next tragedy occurred when I lost my job. All my hard work and the promises made to me resulted in nothing.

At the age of 27 I vowed I would never, ever work for anyone else again and I never did. From this point on, I told myself I would control my own destiny no matter how hard or difficult.

I started my own fire safety business. It expanded rapidly. I travelled all over the world designing fire systems and providing fire training courses for my clients. I had a great company with a fantastic team working for me. Life again was great until another dark Sunday, wintry night that would result in tragedy number 3.

A terrible accident occurred in which I fell through a large, plate glass window. My body within seconds became mutilated by the large pieces of sharp glass tearing my skin apart down to the bone.

Within just a few seconds I was unconscious as blood seeped from multiple wounds all over my body. Minutes later I was in hospital having an emergency operation requiring more than four hundred stitches. After the operation, even more serious problems arose as I suffered a blood clot that nearly killed me.

I could not work, drive or fly in an aircraft for more than six months. All the orders for my company started to dry up and I was forced to sell for the best money I could. I negotiated a good sale and was pleased with myself as I entered the lawyer's office on the day of completion to sign all the documentation. Immediately, tragedy number 4 struck. The purchaser declined to go ahead. In the previous two weeks they had started to steal all my important customers and some of my best staff. I was too busy to notice. Not only were they not proceeding but I had nothing left of any value to sell. I lost my business when it closed. The bank forced me to sell my house and give the profit to them. I was left car less and penniless.

I picked myself up again like a badly wounded boxer who refused to give up. My new company quickly got off the ground. Within years I was back earning more money than ever from not one company, but now three.

Tragedy number 5, however, was looming fast. Two of my co-Directors had formed a fourth company and for six months had slowly siphoned off all the profits and most lucrative sales. I was too busy to see this happening from right under my nose. By the time I found out, all three original companies were in a financially crippled situation and I had no alternative but to put each of them into liquidation. Personally, I again, lost everything.

Totally destroyed both mentally and physically I promised myself that there would not be a future tragedy number 6. In the unlikely event one would try and come I further promised myself that I would be strong enough financially, physically and mentally to withstand any future problems. But how would I do it?

[The 6-Step Coaching Model]

What?	To be a millionaire in less than three years time and be financially independent forever.
Why?	Because it would provide my family with financial security and I would not repeat the stress of previous tragedies.
Who?	For the benefit of myself to make the future of my wife and two young daughters financially secure forever.
Where?	I would implement my plan in new offices close to where I lived with close, loyal business colleagues.
When?	Now. At the age of 46 time was not on my side to be a millionaire by the age of 50. That was one of my teenage goals that has stayed with me.
How?	By hard work, discipline and giving excellent customer service. Maximising at every opportunity sales and profits. Treating my staff as my most valuable business asset. Sell my company for as much money as I could within three years to become a millionaire.

Triumph! The 6-Step Coaching Model worked! At the age of 49, just over a year ago, I became not only a millionaire but have net assets in excess of 1.5 million pounds. My goal is to double this to three million pounds in the next three years and I know I can do it.

You can too. Of all the books I have read and advice I have been given, the 6-Step Coaching Model has been the best to help me achieve my life's main goals and countless others.

John Ellis, LCSi

A contribution by

Ann Fieldhouse

A graduate LCSi – LifeCoach School international
student from England.

Stan was a jovial forty something, always the life and soul of a party, someone everyone was glad to meet. He had been a middle manager of a well known successful telecoms company for a number of years and was rightly proud of his achievement. I was chatting to him one day and mentioned a DVD I had heard about but not yet seen and he volunteered to lend it to me, as he had it nearby in the car. It was about a week later when I returned it to his house that I learned that sadly things were far from happy at home.

I arrived at the house at about ten thirty and rang the doorbell. The family , Betty his wife and four children (three girls and a boy) were not short of the luxuries of life, having an indoor swimming pool and plenty of space. I glanced through the kitchen window and thought I heard a whimper. Trying the door, I found it open and walked in " Betty, are you there? It's Ann. I've brought Stan's DVD back. How are you? Are you alright? " .

" It's Stan," Betty said (I gave her a hug). "He is being so awful. The children run away when he gets home, and Peter is always getting into trouble with the police. He's only fifteen and Stan tells him he can't come home and that he is not good enough. I think he expects too much of him. Stan is very high powered and Peter just isn't that way inclined. My side of the family are much more laid back....I just don't know what to do".

" I tell you what I will do Betty... I haven't brought this DVD back this morning.. I'll come again when Stan is here alone. You work later don't you?. What time do you go to work? Stan will be here on his own for several hours won't he? I will come again this afternoon. Don't worry...things can get better ".

At about two o'clock I arrived again at the house carrying the DVD. I rang the bell and Stan came straight away and invited me in. We sat down and I asked Stan how things were. He said that he was not happy with the way things were going and began to repeat what I had heard from Betty, but from his perspective.

"You say that the way things are, is not how you want them to be. What is it.... you really want?"

" I want to love them all unconditionally. I don't want my family to run away from me. I know Betty is not happy with me. It is just that at work my senior manager is always down on me and I seem to come home and take it out on the family. I really want to love them all unconditionally, because that is the most important thing for me... for Betty, for all of us." Stan was clearly unhappy with himself.

"Stan...you can see clearly how you want things to be, and you really want to love all the family .Your greatest wish is to love them all unconditionally. Why would this be so important to you, do you think?

"I have always put all my energies into being successful, and making a lot of money but what is the point, if my family life is so awful? My only wish now is to make this a really happy and loving family, otherwise I have wasted my life, haven't I ".

" What would you need to do... to change things from the way they are now. To the way you really want them to be?"

"Yes ....it really is what I want,... and I must start to change things now. I realise it will take a while to gain their trust, but it is so important. I am going to get them all together and tell them how sorry I am. I must start now by accepting them all as they are, and by not trying to change them My big mistake has been to want Peter to become a manager. I can see that it is much more important to allow him to do what he wants to do, whatever that may be, and give him all the encouragement he needs. I have a feeling he has been getting into trouble with the police because he can't live up to my expectations. Betty has been worried sick at me telling him not to come home. Oh how awful I have been to him!"

"I am so glad Stan that you can see so clearly what you want and what you need to do. You are right to think it won't happen overnight. Do you think it would help to have a date when you hope to have managed to get into the new habit of accepting everyone...perhaps thirty days?"

"I think I can manage it in twenty days. There is nothing I want more than to break the chain and not come home imposing my manager's attitudes onto my family. I know I can do it'""

"Do you think that it is will be mainly here that the change will take place?"
"Yes mainly, but I think I will take them out more and spend more fun time, with them, so it will be elsewhere as well but mainly here. Oh thank you for coming round and helping me to see my way forward".

Tragically, Stan was killed in a car crash three years later. I never asked how things had progressed but now I heard from Betty that things had become very happy and that Stan had really changed. Today Peter is manager of a restaurant, and all the girls are growing up very balanced, with very happy memories of the last three years of their dad's life.

What a wonderful tool we have in the six step coaching model, which enables a person to get in touch with what they really want, and why, and when and where and how...enabling them to truly change their lives and create a really wonderful future for themselves and those around them! Out of pain- and into triumph.

Anne Fieldhouse, LCSi

afieldhouse@onetel.com

A contribution by

Margaret Haffenden

A graduate LCSi - LifeCoach School international

student from Belgium.

The Breaking of the Wheel

We shall not cease from exploration, and the end of all our exploring will be to arrive where we started and know the place for the first time

T.S. Eliot 'Little Gidding'

We all have our stocktaking experiences. Often these are tied-in with the major age-defined moments when we become 30, 40, and 50 and beyond, and we look at who we think we are and compare this with what we think we have achieved. It's as though we hold up a mirror to ourselves and take time to have a good look at what we see. Sometimes, what we see looking back at us is a bit skewed, a bit lined and fraught, and we wonder if there's something wrong with the glass itself. But occasionally, just occasionally, we can look at our reflections and think: Hmmmm – not bad at all!

I had a reflective moment of this sort recently, in a glass tower in the City of London, when I found myself confronted with rows of people in suits listening to me talk about Emotional Intelligence, teamwork and leadership in a way which I hoped would not evoke the tired and cynical groans of 'Same old Same old'. As I spoke I felt that I was touching them, showing them an unseen door in the high walls which many felt had trapped them, and allowing them to know that there was another place to move to – not by escaping, but by facing up to things within themselves.

For a brief moment I saw myself among them, and remembered how I had been years ago: booted and pin-stripe suited, handsomely paid; lap-top loaded; bags packed and perpetually ready to go, leaving on jet planes and virtually living in cloned hotels in every corner of the known world. Outwardly, I

Becoming a trainer and life coach was a full-time commitment and a big financial investment. Although it is extremely demanding, no-one I know who has done this form of self-development has ever regretted it. In due course I set up my own business in Brussels and proceeded to teach what I loved.

So it was an odd feeling to stand before those shrewd and spirited individuals in that large and futuristic building in the heart of one of the biggest cities on Earth and realise that I had spiralled back toward the world I had once sworn never to revisit. But I use the term 'spiral' exactly, for it was not a case of coming full circle. Instead of one end joining up again to complete the same old wheel, the same old flat and two-dimensional circuit, I felt I was taking the curve upward, into another dimension of my own experience. Revisiting my starting point but from a level above it. I realised that I now had the skills, insight and experience to work with people who wanted to break the wheel before the wheel broke them. Not by leaving their jobs but by understanding themselves and others in a profoundly different way.

As a trainer and life coach, I now combine self mastery and emotional intelligence concepts and use these to underpin personal and team leadership programmes. I also use the 6-Step Model taught by LCSi as an integral part of any programme I deliver. My work takes me to the United Kingdom, to Brussels and to the United States, but, these days, never on the hamster wheel.

Margaret Haffenden, LCSi

m.haffenden@scarlet.be

Belgian mobile: +32 (0)486 470594

UK mobile: +44 (0)7891 309351

A contribution by

Rose Hebborn

A graduate LCSi - LifeCoach School international
student from England.

ESSENCE OF ROSE

The sun was shining, the sky was blue – a beautiful day. I was walking along the cliff path at Budleigh Salterton, where I lived.

So why did I feel so unwell – drained and breathless?

Only three weeks before I had heard my inner voice clearly saying 'You will be ill if you continue living this way.' I did not listen.

I cared for our children Katie and Peter, (seven and a half and four and a half years old) running them to various after school classes. At weekends I used to work on the Neonatal unit in Exeter.

We had eighteen students from our local agricultural college, Bicton, who were staying with us on a bed and breakfast basis. I had help changing the sheets each week but the rest I did myself – running between Otterton, we had ten students there and Budleigh Salterton, where we had eight students with us.

You are possibly thinking, 'This woman must have been mad!' Well our daughter was dyslexic and needed to be in a smaller class to have a better chance of learning – and a private school costs money!

I likened my life to being on an express train, not looking left or right. I needed to STOP, get off and enjoy the view.

I managed to get home from my cliff walk. I took a short cut down hill to make it easier, I decided to see my doctor – he knew there was something wrong with me, but didn't know what.

The following week I was STOPPED. I felt so unwell one day – I staggered to our front gate and collapsed on the pavement. The first person to come to my rescue was a lady suffering with M.E. Myalgic Encephalomyelitis. (also known as Post Viral fatigue Syndrome or Chronic Fatigue Syndrome) Little did I know that day, that this was the illness I had too.

The doctor was called and so was the ambulance. I was admitted to hospital and was asked if I was depressed about anything – the only concern I had was, 'What was wrong with me?'

I was housebound for several months, I thought I was going to die. It felt like someone had got a bicycle pump and sucked every ounce of energy from my body. I had no energy, I was really breathless, my muscles and joints were constantly in pain. My mind was in a complete fog and I couldn't think clearly, concentration was impossible. Allergies seemed to spring from nowhere. My head was pounding along with my heart.

My first thought was 'This kind of thing only happens to other people – I've got two young children I can't be ill.' I quickly realised that all kinds of experiences happen to other people on a daily basis – so why not me.

I thought either I take this as a positive experience in my life or negative. The choice was mine – I felt that this illness was a gift and that I should take this as an opportunity in my life to grow and develop as a person – a whole person.

Immediately I knew that the 'holistic approach' and *incredible self care* would be a vital part of my recovery. I knew that I firstly needed to accept the situation and continue day by day and step by step, however small, working on the whole of me, body, mind and spirit. I remembered that the word disease, *dis-ease* meant a lack of harmony within, I needed to become at peace within and regain my balance. I prayed for guidance – that I was shown what I needed to learn so that I could grow through M.E. and out of it.

I adopted various techniques to release any negative emotions that I felt, i.e. fear, anger, frustration for example, writing, drawing, painting, laughing, and crying – thus leaving my body, mind and spirit at peace to heal.

My first steps included healing, diet, affirmations, meditation, flower remedies, followed by other therapies as I took steadier and firmer steps forward. Most important was me taking responsibility for my health and wellbeing, becoming self empowered, making the right choices for me on my journey of recovery.

My journey through M.E. has been the most enlightening time of my life – my priorities and what is really precious to me, becoming crystal clear, I believe the best things in life are free.

Following the pathway of *incredible self care* was of paramount importance, very gently and gradually healing my body mind and spirit, seeking the root cause, releasing fears, embracing and loving me and living in the moment.

Before I became unwell with M.E. I worked as a State Enrolled Nurse. Part of understanding why this had happened to me, was realising that I had come to a cross roads in my life and the sign post was clear.

I started Rainbow M.E. Support Group n 1991 – a nationally registered holistic group, helping people with M.E. to become aware that the body, mind and spirit are interconnected. To become well entails looking at the whole person. I recovered after two years and wanted to encourage self help and share what I passionately feel is the pathway to recovery.

I have set up a private 'Holistic M.E. Care' consultancy service. Due to the nature of M.E. I offer the choice of one to one appointments or phone consultations –by appointment. I will undertake home visits by special arrangement.

After studying with LCSi – Life Coach School international I am setting up group sessions called 'Essence of You' incorporating the six step coaching model. The aim is to gently empower people who are recovering from M.E. to move forward step by step on their journey, giving them tools and techniques, and encouraging self help, discovering their soul purpose for experiencing the *dis-ease* - so that they can gradually regain their health and wellbeing.

I practice Advanced Structured Hypnotherapy and specialise in working with people with M.E. I am also a qualified complementary therapist and practice Healing CCHA, Aromatherapy IIHHT, Reflexology IIHHT and Therapeutic massage ITEC.

Rose Hebborn, LCSi

Email   Hhebborn @aol.com

www.essenceofrose.co.uk

Rainbow M.E. Support Group www.rainbow-me.org.uk

A contribution by

Marusja Harasymiw

A graduate LCSi - LifeCoach School international
student from England.

THE ANSWERS WITHIN

Mulling over my client's name and birth details, I rapidly experienced an influx information.   Although only in her early thirties, she had an air of defeat about her and appeared older. I perceived a cautious and safe outlook, rather held back and a distinct lack of vibrancy about her person.

Utilising my knowledge of numerology together with a lifelong intuitive perception, I began to relate relevant information to her, helping her to visibly relax from her initial tension.   Despite her practical image I knew that there was a hidden element dying to emerge from within and yet was so suppressed that her life was not enjoyable.

In order to help Jenny to bridge the aching chasm between her seemingly stable, yet uninspired existence and her heart's desire, I needed to give voice to my understanding.

"You are playing safe with your career choice" I spoke gently and wishing to instil encouragement continued.   "You have an artistic talent and should you consider taking up painting, you would do very well."

As always, I was rewarded with an astonished response at the recognition involved in this query.

"I can't believe that you've said that. I would really love to paint portraits of pets."

Jenny was trapped by her decision to work as an accountant; yearning for the day when she could afford to give this up and do what she truly thought would make her happy.

As a result she emanated a rather run down and depleted presence. Although she was adequate and meticulous in her work she did not feel nourished in any way.

In her mind, the obstacle to her fulfilling her wish to be an artist was money.

After an expensive education she had been expected to support herself in a professional and secure financial position. It was deeply integrated into her belief system that it would be impossible to make a living as an artist.

My job at that point in time, after the recognition of her deeply recessed gifts was to help Jenny to look at her options to see if she could open up to her potential.

This was made much easier by the foundation of validity now set. On ascertaining that she had availability at the weekends and that she would be willing to begin the painting work then, whilst holding on to her day job for the time being, she found herself in a win-win, no risk position.

This was a good step and one that she had never considered before. She could function in a climate free of any financial concerns, her income maintained by her day job, so that she could relax and enjoy an easy transition into her dream job.

Only three months later, Jenny had relinquished her accountancy practice completely and on the strength of her accelerating success in pet portraiture had transcended her fears and ventured into her favoured profession on a full time basis.

She called me expressing her immense appreciation at this transition, saying that she would never have had the courage to accomplish this without the coaching which we embarked upon.

It gives me a great deal of pleasure to witness any individual finding promotion in their life and my part in this is simply as a cog in the wheel, enabling the machinery to go round again. In this case, I was also gratified that Jenny had trusted herself sufficiently to follow through.

On another occasion, a young man came to me in some distress as his business partner had abused the trust between them and was discovered to be carrying out contracts behind his back, not passing over moneys due.

On analysis it became evident that this was an opportunity for my client. The partner was not acting in a 'partnering' manner and the relationship was not affording Ken the support either emotionally or financially that he had hoped for. What did transpire, however, was that Ken was quite capable of going it alone and we devised a strategy to help him do so with more confidence.

With delight, I heard from him soon after that he had set up his own business and was managing perfectly well on his own and prospering.

Through countless people approaching me for assistance over the years, I have in turn listened, observed, studied and sought to engage in the most helpful ways that I can.

I truly believe in the word 'can' and the element of my work that inspires others to find clarity and to raise their expectations arises from an acute depth of experience and a desire to be of service.

Since early childhood I have witnessed pain on so many levels and somehow have managed to seek to comfort those in distress. Within my own life I have been presented with a veritable minefield of obstacles and have defined and refined an array of techniques in order to transcend these.

Personal Growth is now an industry and yet to me it is merely a natural inclination.

After all, if one examines nature it is obvious that plants reach towards the light to achieve growth and each and every one of us houses such a template to function from.

As technology speeds up the process and availability of information gathering, one of the most challenging things to deal with is choice.

What may be overlooked is that as advances are made in these areas, we as human beings retain information which has not changed over time. This inner knowledge is often forgotten and hidden and there is a tendency to rely on external material which may or may not gel with our inner selves.

A major contribution in resolving this imbalance is in the arena of Life Coaching, because of the ease in which clarification can occur. It is essentially a practical approach, offering anyone in need a way forward out of dilemma and provides momentum towards goals using highly effective tools.

For example, PaTrisha-Anne Todd, the founder of LCSI has devised *The 6-Step Coaching Model* to create a specific technique which is rather like a search engine, only in this respect it is for finding out the answers to questions from within.

The utilisation of Life Coaching reflects a great need in society today for a certain quality of guidance, previously confined to sporting activities, but now carrying over into everyday concerns and is a welcome addition in both personal and corporate fields.

Marusja Harasymiw, LCSi

Marusja began developing her practice in the 1980's after extensive study relating to Psychotherapeutic Procedures, Meditative Techniques and various forms of Healing. Her background as a naturally inclined Intuitive has enabled her to provide a unique Life Coaching Methodology, assisting people from many walks of life to find their own potency towards fulfilment and happiness.

As an Advanced Hypnotherapist she is able to help those wishing to change habits and live healthier lives. As a Silvamethod Instructor she is able to help people to use their minds more effectively.

She also holds workshops on a regular basis and lectures widely to incorporate and convey what she has learnt in group settings.

www.gratefulminds.co.uk   Email: marusja@gratefulminds.co.uk

Tel: 01623 411123

A contribution by

Francelyn Lewis

A graduate LCSi - Lifecoach School international
student from the Caribbean and currently in London.

Be grateful and live your life, DO YOUR BEST
For only you can live YOUR LIFE.
Live your life NOW!
Do not wait for tomorrow, for Today is a BLESSING!

Each of our lives tells a story. Sometimes we do take our lives for granted until we become aware of how precious it is. Be grateful for each day. At times it takes significant events for us to realise how blessed we are.

For over twenty-five years, I believed that my life was wonderful even though I'd had my ups and downs like most people. I had a wonderful caring husband, a loving, giving daughter and lived in a beautiful home on a fantastic tropical island. But something vital was missing.

Ten years ago my life went through a rough patch. I realised that not only was I being taken for granted but that I was being controlled by my husband. What I had thought of as loving attention for so many years, was in fact the actions of a selfish and self-centred individual. This situation continued to deteriorate into what I called at the time: 'silent treatment', which I later found out was in fact a form of verbal abuse. Nothing was ever good enough and every situation resulted in arguments and high tension levels.

In what seemed to be a blink of an eye, this situation deteriorated even further and soon it was impossible to have any form of discussions without a barrage of profanities being aimed at me. High levels of stress were draining my every strength and I began suffering from emotional distress.

By this time, my husband was always angry and totally out of control. The only time he was civil, was when he wanted financial help and even this eventually broke down when he started demanding money for his personal needs. If I was unable to comply with his requests, he became threatening and eventually violent.

Now, I have always been a praying person but by this time I was asking "Why me Lord?", "What is really happening here?" Even though the situation worsened progressively, through prayer I eventually realised that I had to make a choice – to survive or not; I had to get away from this situation. It was a matter of having to leave everything I had worked and sacrificed for over many years. This was a major decision but one that simply had to be made for both my sanity and my life. I had come to realise that these were worth more than relationships or material things.

Most of us live each day and are not aware of who we are or why we exist. We go through life wondering what's next. Life is a journey and it's up to us to seek guidance (be it from our faith or from the Higher Power in which we believe) to find out where we are going, how to get there and what's expected of us when we do get there. Each area of our lives has consequences and we need to make a plan and take action to get what we want in life.

To achieve balanced lives, we need to carry out copious amounts of self care. We must know, love and understand ourselves as individuals, maintain positive thoughts and peace of mind about every situation in which we find ourselves. Everyone experiences challenges in life but we must be able to take each situation as it comes and turn it to our advantage. By approaching each situation in this way, we become stronger individuals and move closer towards achieving success and better lives. We need to remember that we are what we think – if we think negative thoughts, they do tend to materialise.

We are all unique individuals no matter what we look like or where we are from. The Higher Power has made each of us for some especially significant purpose, which will be revealed to us at the right time and place. In the meantime, we must be patient and learn to develop and trust our intuition.

When we learn to trust and love ourselves, we learn to forgive others who have hurt us along the way. This helps us learn to forgive ourselves – whether it is for not trusting our instincts or simply for not loving ourselves enough to leave difficult situations behind. When we do not forgive – be it ourselves or others, this tends to manifest in us as stress, burdens and dis-ease.

It's been over five years since I choose to leave this situation behind me. I've taken responsibility for my life and returned to the UK to restart my life. I have a new home and an even more fulfilling career. I am a firm believer that as you give, so shall you receive. My entire career to date has surrounded helping others and this has grown significantly over the last five years, as I've helped final year dental students achieve their goals.

We all need inspiration and motivation at times and I am thankful that I can be of service to my students, colleagues, family and friends when they need encouragement to move forward. I guess it is not surprising that I found my way to becoming a qualified Life Coach, which helps me to carry on helping others fulfil their dreams.

When I reflect to ten years ago, my achievements are nothing short of a miracle. I have grown both personally and spiritually. I've moved on and firmly believe that this has been possible due to the courage and strength received from God's blessings.

Life is wonderful gift. Follow your dreams to your destiny and do what feels good in your heart and success will be yours. Always remember that all things are possible for those who believe.

I hope my story has inspired you in some way. You can contact me to discuss overcoming life's obstacles and achieving your goals at:

Francelyn Lewis, LCSi

HarmoneeRose LifeCoaching Concepts
P. O. Box 51631
London SE8 5WH
Telephone: 0800 633 5996
Mobile: 0784 720 2903
Email: harmoneerose@yahoo.co.uk

MY STORIES OF INSPIRATION, COURAGE, AND DETERMINATION

AN ANTIDOTE TO CLICHÉ

"It takes a lot of courage to release the familiar and the seemingly secure, to embrace the new. But there is no real security in what is no longer meaningful. There is more security in the adventurous and exciting, for in movement there is life, and in change there is power." *Alan Cohen*

The expression, 'Wake-Up Call', has become a cliché. It is overused and undervalued on the streets and in the media. It has slipped into our vocabulary without depth or reverence. We fail to acknowledge that Life is eternally benevolent and 'wake-up calls' happen several times a day. Some are subtle yet powerful and some catapult us on a life changing trajectory of which we could never have imagined. I want to share a 'wake-up call' that changed my life forever; gave me focus and shook the complacency out of me.

I was studying my BCom (Bachelor of Commerce degree), and had been easing my way through it, as most young men of some privilege can. I knew I needed to graduate to get out into the work-place, but I wasn't really motivated towards completion. I had also managed to be accepted into an MBA (Master of Business Administration), despite the fact that I had not yet completed my BCom, nor had the relevant years of experience usually required for acceptance. The MBA inspired me a little more, but still, there was no real passion - I was primarily driven by the higher income and status that the MBA would potentially provide. I was living with my father and he was supporting me financially. He always told me that I could do anything I wanted, but to be honest, there was nothing I found particularly inspiring. I was in a contented dream world, a blind optimist. I was not afraid of the future because I actually did everything I could from staring honestly into it.

I left the house in the morning to head for the gym – vanity and youth somehow allowed time and energy for heavy workouts. I kissed my dad goodbye and told him I would see him later. When I arrived home I found my, I entered our home to find my father down on the ground. My Step-mother and gardener were struggling to lift him up. It was of course impossible to recognise the 'wake-up call' already surging through my veins – altering brain chemistry forever and asking primal instincts from a complacent man. My body wisdom kicked in and I carried him to the car.

The phone was not working and an ambulance would take too long. I sped – driving skilfully, with razor sharp focus - one simple intention – the art of presence that I would so often try to recapture in later years. My father I am sure felt that surge of energy, that potential, something roar inside of me even if I didn't in that moment. The doctors took him from us; we were to wait outside; to play the scene from a thousand film and TV shows. It is impossible to stereotype your own private torture. It might have looked the same to any audience but my internal landscape was as bleak as it was unique.

I was terrified to lose him. My future had me by the throat as I struggled to plead in prayer, something I had never done before. I did not know to whom I asked to save his life, to keep him for me, to have the chance to see our futures together. But the wake-up call was in motion and my prayers were part of it. Then the doctor warmly and coldly, the way recent death is, simply said, "There was nothing we could do . . . I'm sorry." We went inside to say our 'goodbyes', things mostly felt and not spoken. How ill equipped I was with one of Life's greatest certainties!

I went into a place of extreme stillness – total silence within me - nothing mattered and time stood still. Friends and family came and went and played their parts admirably and I looked out at the audience vacantly.

In the ensuing days the other great certainty arrived, expected and unwelcome, Taxes. My father's estate was frozen. Debtors and Creditors determined. Taxes paid. Suddenly, it hit me; my "life-line" was cut off. My father was supporting me whilst he was alive and now there was no financial support at all. All avenues were explored – I was finally 'financially independent' without a cent.

My mother did the only thing she could by becoming a guarantor on a bank loan to tied me over for 4 months to help aid with my studies. Family friends who

owned a computer institute offered me an intensive IT training course. After 4 month of intensive study I would be guaranteed a job in the then burgeoning IT industry. Somewhere inside, it felt like eating humble pie on a not so silver spoon.

I knew I was in trouble and I was getting desperate. Often with the death of a parent or the birth of your first child; your wake-up call almost whispers, *"It's time to grow up – be self responsible and be responsible for enjoying all that that entails."* I realised I needed to act, to do something to change MY attitude towards what I considered to be Life beating me down.

[The 6-Step Coaching Model]

What?

I wanted to get a completed qualification to enable me to gain employment that paid well and that I enjoyed. I also needed to pay back the loan.

Why?

This was more than just basic survival. Yes, I needed to survive. But somewhere I recognised that adrenalin surge to take responsibility of my life, my destiny and to choose how I optimistically and appropriately handled anything that life threw my way. I did not like playing the victim and freedom pointed to self-responsibility. This was not measured by success at this stage but simply taking ACTION.

When?

I needed to act immediately. I had 4 months of money to survive and my training was also 4 months. I learned a great lesson in how deadlines and urgency can be a great motivator but only if you make friends with them first.

Who?

I needed help to achieve my targets. I gratefully accepted my mother's offer to sign surety for me on the bank loan, and also the offer to do IT training. I needed the emotional support of family and friends to help the grieving process and also support for the intense period ahead. I could see this path would benefit my family and friends as well as me. I started to feel more confident in what I had to offer the world, what society could benefit from my contribution: for the first time I could feel a sense of purpose. I could feel this 'wake-up call' turning from a neglected cliché into a character building experience.

Where?

To achieve my goal, I would have to 'turn up' at the computer institute (IT training) each and every day – committed and willing. Everyday I pictured where I would be with this steadfast approach: Receiving my IT qualification and then being gainfully employed in an IT role that paid well and that I enjoyed

How?

In order to achieve my goal, I had to do all the following:

- Get the Bank Loan
- Sign up for the training
- Believe that I could do it and change victim-hood into self-responsibility
- Dedicate myself and commit to doing whatever it took to successfully complete the training.
- NEVER give up
- Apply for suitable job vacancies
- Go for interviews and get job offers
- Select the job that mutually satisfied my potential employer and myself
- Start working

The computer Institute's training was the most intensive program I have ever attended (even to this day). The course was of a high standard with hours of homework, theory and the learning of new concepts, code, and computer language. I lost my weekends and evenings to revision for weekly examinations. I was un-recognisable to myself and yet even amid the stress and exhaustion I began to feel a sense of achievement and pride. Again, I could see clearly that my attitude towards my studies was my best friend. When it felt too much and too hard and I had collapsed into that old victim mould I would try to find the joy and play in the greatest challenges. I became determined and yet honouring of my emotional self. I could stand up out of the collapse and still see that it was a difficult time but not impossible.

I was invigorated by this new way of thinking – my mind liked its new mapping and gave me the brilliant idea of completing both the IT course and my Bcom. With empowering thoughts of distinguishing myself I was able to continue effortlessly. My grades improved and so did my general well being. I received both my qualifications and set myself on paper as a unique graduate. I had an interview with a small yet very well respected consulting company. Intuitively I knew that this position was right for me. I passed the interview and gratefully accepted my first 'grown-up' job. My goals had been achieved and I had gained so much more.

Every morning I now make it a practice to ask that I have the presence and vigilance to see clearly my 'wake-up' calls great and small. To be guided effortlessly through their teachings to my next step and the next step and so on. Right action is assured with presence and vigilance. The antidote to cliché is simply bringing awareness and a little of your precious time for contemplation on 'what just happened?' and "what am I going to do about it?" In some strange way I am happy to have been focused, present, vigilant and taking appropriate swift action in the last few moments that I shared with my father. Before he passed he did get to see the best in me and in his passing I became a man.

And more...

THE IRONY OF HABIT AND ROUTINE

Most of us wait for something dramatic to effect change in our lives albeit most of the time subconscious. We often hear statements about having to hit rock bottom, having to lose everything, a near-death experience forcing us to re-evaluate our life-style priority plan etc. Or we are so busy with where we want to be and frustrated with where we actually are that we become anxious and *'future'* driven. Yet the most steadfast way towards change in the direction that *you* want is simply habit. Habit and routine are the foundation that your commitment can build upon.

I was working for a Sydney-based IT consultancy for some time and was currently posted to a project in Darwin, Northern Australia. I was on a career path that was slowing down and I wanted to move into a more challenging IT Architect role. The way forward was with new, emerging cutting-edge technologies. My employers had not acquired any contracts that would allow me to transition in the way I wanted. I became bored and frustrated with my unchallenging work schedule. I knew that I had to keep my intention at the forefront of my mind and also keep the habit and the routine of working, social life, exercise, eating well, hobbies, striving to do my best – all whilst actively looking for a way to change tracks. My daily routine kept me sane and actually gave me time, space, energy and financial stability to scout for new opportunities.

I was given a flyer for an introductory seminar on wealth creation and felt a strong pull towards it. Naturally, I was interested in wealth creation for all the obvious reasons but most importantly I could buy some financial freedom. A friend and I drove along the street on the morning of the seminar and were battling to find the venue. After 10 minutes being lost my interest disappeared and I became exceptionally frustrated. I just wanted to go home. It was fascinating to see how quickly my frustration with my present life unashamedly rose to the surface stamping its feet like a child. There is something about being witnessed in all of this that solidifies it into a harsh reality. My friend, the convivial witness, convinced me to have one more try and I resentfully agreed.

The introductory seminar started, and I was hooked almost from the start. We were challenged to think in new ways. Renowned entrepreneurs, authors and motivational speakers were quoted. We analysed our financial status, our forecasts within dream vs. reality strategies, potential earnings, markets and trends – the usual suspects at a wealth seminar. But to my fresh ears it was exciting and empowering. Then came the 'crunch'. The 5 day programme would cost approximately AU$5,000. My doubtful mind was busy with justifying 'losing' this amount when I had come to 'gain' money. Yet, somehow it was bigger than me and I signed up on the spot. There was an interesting guarantee which I would later come to understand and appreciate – there would be a full refund for dissatisfied participants but only if they had completed the whole course.

I thought the course was going to be 5 days of Finance, Money, Investments, Options, Futures, and property, but we ended up spending the first 3 days really focusing inside of ourselves to what we really wanted and why, to what was really important in our lives. We didn't even come close to the topics I had thought we would cover. I had some amazing 'break-through's' and self-realisations in those 3 days, and even ended up with my mission statement – my life's purpose. Eventually we concluded with 2 days of the topics I had anticipated – great information and strategies. But for me, paling into insignificance compared to the previous 3 days.

One of the most valuable tools was a simple goals sheet - identifying my most important goals for the next 30 days. My number 1 goal was to have a new job within 30 days in which I would be stimulated and challenged that would advance my career working in and with 'cutting-edge' technologies. We were told to carry this sheet with us, reading it several times per day throughout the day. I don't recall exactly, but I think I may even have repeated it up to 150 times in a single day. I made my commitment, and the 'habit' of repeating this mantra part of my daily routine.

[The 6-Step Coaching Model]

What?

I wanted a new job in which I could advance both professionally and personally working with new, emerging cutting-edge technologies.

Why?

I was stuck and frustrated with my present work life. I wanted a challenge and continue seeking and growing in life. I really enjoyed new technologies.

When?

I wanted it within 30 days! I would know I had it when I had signed the job contract.

Who?

I wanted it for myself - for my own growth and 'sanity'. Indirectly, others around me would benefit because I would be less frustrated and more positive. I had no idea who could help me – but I made a commitment to be available for research and networking.

Where?

I knew I wanted to remain in Sydney, Australia and preferably not too far from where I was already working.

How?

I was not sure exactly how I was going to find my new job, but my plan was to:

- Go on-line and start searching for jobs

- Contact some recruiters

- Continue to read my goals out several times throughout the day and continue my daily routine that kept order and stability rewarding me with time, space, energy and financial stability to scout for new opportunities.

Within 3 days I received a call from someone who I had worked with on a previous project. He had recently joined an emerging Telecommunications company in Australia and had been asked to create a team that would work for him. In that instant, I knew I would be working for him. He told me a little about the role and asked me if I was interested. "Yes" I said. He thought I was saying "Yes" about being interested, but actually, I was saying "Yes" to the job offer he had not yet made. He invited me to breakfast to discuss it further, went into a little more detail, and again I said "Yes". "Don't you want to think it over?" he asked, surprised that I appeared to be jumping in feet first. I agreed to think it over, but for me that was simply getting clear on job description, salary, contracts etc. A month later, I was working as an IT OSS Architect towards the first roll-out of 3G in Australia and one of the first in the world on a considerably higher salary than I had previously been earning or had expected to earn.

I was committed to the goal and flexible with the approach – the approach is not the goal. My 'WHY' was certainly big enough and I had laid my commitment on the foundation of daily routine and habit to give me stability and security and I trusted that the 'HOW' would show up. I learned that it is great to make plans but not to get too attached to them – a good plan has room for evolvement. Ironically, the anchor of habit and routine gave me the flexibility and freedom to manifest my goal.

And more…

FAITH IN FORMING A FAMILY (Life has a sense of humour)

Like many young ambitious men, somewhere in my distant planning, I knew I wanted a family. However, I did not realise that my beliefs around women, commitment and family would be continually shaped through my experience and what Life continually offered me. What I had imagined and what Life finally offered me were very different – thankfully I learned to be open, flexible and curious.

I had always been afraid of commitment. It meant only one thing – entrapment – a place where I would lose my sense of self, ambitions, drive and focus. I had had several relationships with women from different countries and cultural backgrounds. Although I had dated a few blondes, I had a preference for brunettes and if I am honest, when thinking about a partner I was sure that she would not be an English woman.

In February 2002 during an 'Advanced Skills' workshop I noticed one of the trainers, Amba, whom I thought was attractive, though not usually my 'type' and I didn't give her any more thought.

A couple of weeks later I attended a 'Manifest Abundance Seminar'; where we analysed negative belief systems that were holding us back from living our chosen life-path; where we sabotaged our potential and how and when they were 'conditioned' in our mind map. Part of the seminar focused on visioning – in a sense, similar to goal setting, but executed more with a combined meditative 'open heart' space as well as 'mind space'. One of my new 'goals' was to have my own family within 2 years; a wife and children. Amba was again on staff for this retreat.

[The 6-Step Coaching Model]

What?
I wanted to find my wife and have children.

Why?
I wanted someone to share and compliment my life: someone with the same ideals and capacity for potential and vision; a symbiotic relationship of mutual support, love and respect; someone to grow with, to laugh with and to cry with. I wanted to be a loving, guiding and loved father.

When?
I wanted to have this within 2 years.

Who?
I wanted it personally, and it was no-one else's decision. The only other person that would need to be directly involved would be my future wife.

Where?
I was used to working and studying in various countries and had no attachment to a specific location for this particular goal. . I was simply present and open to having it in my life.

How?
In order to achieve my goal, I had to do the following:

- Put out my intention/goal, and believe it could and would happen

- Stay open, curious and watchful

- Commit to overcome any fear of commitment or losing my 'space'

- Being 'present' and keeping the intention alive

- Trust that it would unfold if I remained focused on my intention

In April 2002, I attended a 'No Ego' retreat. It was a life-changing event for me – so revealing, so enlightening, so freeing. During this week I also kept my other goals alive and the goal intention strong. Toward the end of the week, I was talking to one of the other trainers, who asked me directly what I thought of Amba. I told him she was beautiful and that I was really interested in her, but that I thought it wouldn't be appropriate, because she was a trainer and I was a 'student'. I don't recall his exact words, but in essence, he told me that that was nonsense, and that I should drop those beliefs and take immediate action.

Amba and I really connected. It was beautiful and liberating. Before the end of the seminar, she invited me to come and spend 3 days with her in Sydney before she carried on touring the world with her work. Immediately I agreed. We spent the most amazing 3 days together, passionately making love, being totally open and present with one another.

On our last evening together we were on the beach. I looked at her, and all I could see was beauty and all I could feel was love. I realised that I may never see her again, and then the words just came out of me, "Would you marry me?" "Yes", she said. I felt the fear of commitment begin to kick in, but the excitement and love dissolved the fear.

I hadn't known it at the time, but Amba had also wanted to get married, become a mother, and start a family. Our ideals, goals, vision and dedication to fulfilling our
individual potential as a team matched perfectly. The humorous part was that Amba was both blond and English. She did not fit my 'type'. Again, a great lesson for me in always re-choosing beliefs, asking, "Do these beliefs still serve me or are they old fixed habits?"

Amba continued to travel the world with her work for 3 months. During this time we profited from technology; e-mail, phone calls, postcards, etc, but never being able to see or touch one another. The distance and the longing became unbearable, after 3 months, she resigned from her job, returned to Australia, and we moved in together.

We had planned to get married a few months later and then to have children. By November 2002, however, despite not being married, we felt ready to consciously have a baby. Parenting was something we discussed and planned at great length. The first time we made love after consciously choosing to have a child I felt the old fear return. I knew that that moment would change my life forever. I was afraid. "If it's for our highest and best, if it's for our highest and best", I mantra like repeated. Amba immediately fell pregnant.

Again, fear came, but this time, it was far more furious. It was so incredibly intense, I felt like I was being trapped – like I couldn't escape. It felt like the end of my life – the end of my freedom. I was TERRIFIED. I begged and pleaded "Please, please help me. Please give me strength and courage. I'm so afraid; so very frightened. It feels like the end of my life. Please help me. I don't know what's going to happen, or how this is going to change my life, but please help me!!" I cried and released so much energy. Again and again, the fear came; again and again I pleaded for strength, courage, and help.

Somehow this experience felt like my right of passage to being a father, to really saying YES to this new human being – metaphorically it felt comparable to Amba's intense and challenging labour. On the 28th of August 2003, our son Max was born. Those first few days and weeks were surreal. I had to keep 'checking in' with myself to stay grounded as the reality of this little miracle of baby and family penetrated deep into my heart. My vision, my dream, my goal had morphed into 'our vision, our dream, our goal' and I was perfectly happy losing 'myself' and surrendering to Life's little miracles.

Anthony Matthews, LCSi

Lead The Change

www.LeadTheChange.com

Info@LeadTheChange.com

A contribution by

Simran Ranu

A graduate LCSi - LifeCoach School international
student from England.

WHO
[An open question containing who is part of t he 6-Step Coaching Model strategy]

With hardly any support from family, totally isolated, with only tears as my consolation, I found my Faith in God was the only thing that kept me strong. My best friends of 15 years, and my dear Aunt Taro, were my only support, and my redeemers.

WHY
[An open question containing why is part of t he 6-Step Coaching Model strategy]

Poverty is a call for action for the poor and the less privileged alike.

An endurance strategy was needed fast! It's easier said than done, but survival is more "Crucial than loosing hope"! I was a Life Coach, I knew I had to act immediately, logically, with a Positive Mental Attitude" or we would not survive. I wasn't prepared to suffer a life time of poverty which could even lead to mental health - depression.

What I wasn't going to allow was FEAR to overtake my mind and emotions.

"Fear" acronym meaning: "A False Estimation Appearing as Real."
I sanctioned my Mind into being Fearless no matter what other complexities arose I was not going to be defeated.

Financed by my friend, I enrolled onto a Doctoral degree. Having no studying space, no PC, I had to study at the local library, who only allowed a certain time a day for usage of their computers. No words can describe the hell I endured during this period of living and studying.

WHAT

[An open question containing what is part of t he 6-Step Coaching Model strategy]

What was required next were rational rules:

Plan the time required for aims, goals, objectives realistically, include short term, long term goals in your plans.
Add dates so you can target yourself on a daily basis.

Time Management   -
Find out how much your Time is worth.
80% of distracted effort produces only   20%   efforts.

Stress Management -
Keep a Stress Diary - Be familiar with the short-term pressure in your life.

Problem Solving - Write down all the problems. Then start to break down into small manageable parts.

Decision Making - Choosing which changes to make, weighing the pros and cons of your decisions, looking at all points of view including financial

Memory Improvement - Run a mental visualisation of your forthcoming successes in your mind until you no longer have any fears. In these visualisations, see yourself handling everything with a sense of courage.

You have three parts to complete: The beginning - your dream, the middle - reaching your desired goals, aims, objectives and the end - dream completed.

WHEN
[An open question containing when is part of t he 6-Step Coaching Model strategy]

Life turns into a game, you need to become the Game!

The principle is competing against you.

It's about self-improvement, about being better than you were.

HOW
[Part of t he 6-Step Coaching Model strategy contains the how element]

I overcame the obstacles in my Life with Life Coach Tools and so can you.

Note :
It is not always necessary to use all five **w** questions when working with *The 6-Step Coaching Model*. The system of the model is a working framework.

10 RULES FOR BOUNCING BACK

1. Despite your life's challenges you are not defeated until you believe you are.

2. Stop procrastinating, start your journey towards having better prospects in health, wealth, career, finance, relationships.

3. If you feel you will succeed or fail, you will. You are the master of your own destiny.

4. There is always someone else who has greater confines in their lives than you have. With determination, you can prove to yourself that you can succeed.

5. Be honest and admit you know what you really want, no day dreaming, or unrealism, then put those specific goals down in writing and develop a plan to achieve them.

6. Each day, view your written goals so that you are focused and clear on what you have to do.

7. Anything you feel worth having or achieving will come only as the result of hard work, motivation, perseverance, continuous learning and belief in yourself.

8. Be logical when it comes to perfecting your new life style. Don't let your heart rule your head. Keep a balance, be clear in decision making.

9. Passion is the key to achieving your desired goals, as are alertness, confidence, optimism, commitment, diligence and ability to accept and learn from criticism.

10. There's no time like the present... what are you waiting for, start now become the "Dreams" instead of just dreaming.

I became my dream, and so can all of you.

I graduated as a Doctor of Metaphysics and am now doing a PhD.

Finally I would like to ask you all to take a moment and remember this one golden rule, of forgiveness, for yourself and others, which, if applied and integrated into your lives with real wisdom, will give you freedom to enjoy life without any limitations:

The wise forgive the unwise and, suffer no loss for it!   _Lord Krishana_

Simran Ranu, LCSi

www.divinesoul.co.uk

www.londoncounselling.net

How to Become

Your Own Life Coach

7 days to a New You!

A seven day journey of self-discovery turning your desires and dreams into reality. Discovering how you can create a compelling future.

The Mini-Course

This part of the book is a special stand alone mini self-coaching course to help you capture your true self and activate your own Personal Performance.

7 Days To A New You!

Research suggests the most effective way to take control of your life and live the lifestyle of your dreams is to know more about yourself. This mini self-coaching course is your self help guide to begin to understand your pattern of thinking and to formulate a realistic action plan, known fondly as the - *'blue print'*. The course is all about you, be honest with yourself and answer the questions from your heart. Just take a look around you of those successful people you admire and their companies. Did you know that their success was once upon a time just a thought, just an idea to do something different. You can achieve your success.

To know about your integral strengths and weaknesses which give you the edge to plotting and developing powerful strategies to create the life you desire and the lifestyle you truly deserve.

You can work through the following pages and begin to plot your journey step by step to Personal Performance excellence in a seven day process. The advanced porgramme is the ninety day programme to take you to your limits. You will discover great things about a very great person, that person is you!

Further more to that end I would like to invite you to stretch your imagination, stir your desires and wants and fire your motivation to step out of your comfort zone and into your Personal Performance A-Z – Achievement Zone!

After you have completed the course and you'd like to take your personal coaching further you can contact me at LCSi.

<u>info@lifecoachschoolinternational.co.uk</u>

or call and leave your contact details +44 (0)1202 389998.

We can then discuss how best to take your achievements further.

Take action towards your goals and do it now.

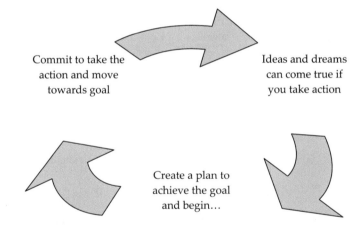

Commit to take the
action and move
towards goal

Ideas and dreams
can come true if
you take action

Create a plan to
achieve the goal
and begin…

Think about this, if you had a magic wand and you could have your dreams and wishes come true what would you wish for? Do you really know what you want and more importantly why you want what you think you want?

Now ask yourself the following; *Why do I do what I do?*

Better still get yourself a journal – the PPCA-Z journal, and write your answers down. It's a proven fact that writing down goals/dreams/ideas and plotting how to achieve them works and actually helps to deliver the goal. Achievement is available to those who truly desire to take their life style to the next level. Once you have a clear vision you can begin to develop your life and step forward and grow through your own efforts. Write it down, use the chart as a guide.

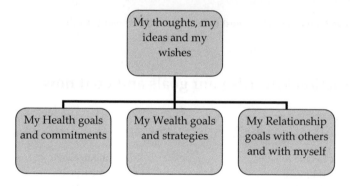

Today is the beginning of another chapter in your lifestyle.

Today you set in motion a far-reaching action plan to raise your standards.

Pick up your PPCA-Z journal, open it and write in today's date.

Now write your autobiography. That's right, write down your life story up to the current time. Include your memories of childhood, growing up and adulthood. Then write about where you are today and where you would like to be in ten years from now. Include a typical day in your new life, where you live and work, your style of home, with whom you live, where you spend your holidays, if you are involved in a church and charity work write that too.

1. How passionate are you about your life and the level of lifestyle that you currently live?

2. How about your self-development? Do you take daily action towards your goals and aspirations?

3. How strongly do you believe that folk like yourself can be stirred into taking habitual positive action towards those dreams and ambitions that lurk somewhere in the back of the mind?

Review your autobiography – Day 1

Did you include the three points above? Did you explain about your passion and hunger to achieve more in your life? Can you confirm that you take daily action towards your goals. Do you know what that action is? Do you firmly believe that you can change a habit of a lifetime for a more desirable outcome. Yes you can if you want to.

Goal Setting – Day 2

I have just asked you to write your autobiography, now let's set your goals. Goals are just ideas/day dreams/positive thoughts until you decide to do something about achieving them, then they become real goals. Goals are a list of wants and desires. So, the only thing that is holding you back from grasping those goals and making them real is your own limiting thoughts.

If you have already listed your goals, and I hope you have within your autobiography, then you can honestly ask yourself, *what do I need to change to set the wheels in motion and achieve a workable plan to reach my goals?*

Goals List – achievement plan

Re-write your goals in your PPCA-Z journal. They may be different now from you wrote before, only because you now know 'why' you want those goals.

Next re-list them in order of importance and priority to you.

Now, re-organise that list into the three sections;

- Health
- Wealth
- Relationships

You might be thinking to yourself. *My goals don't fit into any of the three sections PaTrisha-Anne has just mentioned. What do I do now?*

Actually, you'll find that all your goals do fit into the three sections I've given you. Those three areas of your life actually cover your whole lifestyle.

How can that be? You ask, not quite believing me.

This is how, I'll explain. Say for example you would like to drop some weight, that goal would slot into the health section, or maybe you would like to meet your perfect life long partner, that desire slots into the relationships section, even if you are thinking that your self-esteem and confidence needs a boost that too is a goal that would slot into your relationships section. You need to have a healthy regard for yourself before you can project your personality towards finding a life partner. A wealth goal could be to buy your own home, or to start your own business or perhaps to gain promotion at work. Do you see the picture emerging?

SWOT analysis – Day 3

A SWOT analysis matrix is an insightful tool that will help you to find your hidden talents which in turn will help you take best advantage of all future opportunities and decide exactly what you want to do in life, in your work and income areas. That's all part of the strategy of the seven day new you process. All of which gives you a dynamic *Circle of Life* [another great tool which I speak about a little further on].

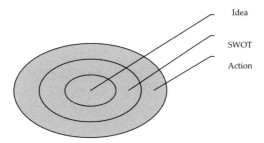

Idea

SWOT

Action

SWOT is used regularly in the corporate domain. We will adopt it to help you analyse and evaluate what talents you have and how best you can use them.

This tool will help you to take action that is currently realistic and promotes a positive relationship within yourself and your outer world. I mention this because throughout my professional coaching career I have helped others achieve their dreams, and be clear about their ambitions. I've helped them to plot attainable goals because they know *why* they want a specific goal. It is this unique positive understanding of self that promotes personal success.

It's your turn to SWOT your life. Use a fresh page in your PPCA-Z journal and SWOT.

How to use the SWOT tool.

The letter S is for _Strengths_ (some of your characteristics might fall into this category), ask yourself the following questions and write down your answers in your PPCA-Z journal, don't forget to date the exercise;

1. What do I do best?
2. What is so unique and special about the way I live my life, speak with others and do my work?
3. What strength is it that other people recognise in me?

The letter W is for _Weaknesses_

1. What area in my life would I live to improve?
2. Where do I fall down in my actions?
3. What weakness is it that other people recognise in me?

Give this area some thought. Ask yourself if other's have mentioned weaknesses to you that you have not recognized? Do you need to _face up to the truth_? Whatever that may be.

The letter O is for *Opportunities*

1. How often do you notice opportunities coming your way?
2. What is currently 'flavour of the month' in other words have you noticed any interesting trends that would be of benefit to you, an opportunity!

While evaluating your opportunities also take into account your weaknesses and strengths. Is there some specific action you could take to create an opportunity for yourself?

The letter T is for *Threats*

1. Do any of the people around you act against you?
2. Are the actions you undertake on a daily basis a threat to you?
3. Are you up to speed with IT?

Analyse any threats in your current lifestyle will help you pin point what you need to do to live a danger free lifestyle, within reason.

Once you have done a SWOT on your life you'll have an insight into how you can design a great life for your self and for those whom you love. The SWOT will help you to be honest with yourself. You won't need to wait anymore; you can create your own lifestyle by being more proactive and recognise opportunities as they pop up in your life. You'll become your own catalyst.

The SWOT tool is a great eye opener to defining what you think about yourself. It will help you to empower yourself and take charge of your life.

THE 10% CLUB – Day 4

Will power is all about having the strength to make a choice. It has nothing to do with anyone or anything else. It's a 100% self choice, which is the foundation of proactive growth and self actualization of desire.

By choosing to choose positively and realistically you develop an effective self management system. Basically, you are self managing yourself. Regrettably there are individuals who choose to not manage themselves and put the blame onto others and use their current situation as an excuse and a chance to procrastinate. Are you one of those?

A good habit to have is to form that habit of 'choice'. It's not difficult once you decide to decide to choose. It's all part of your character building and integrity. It's the motivated individuals who make things happen. They also create what they truly want in life by focusing in a realistic way.

They go the extra mile. Which makes them extra-ordinary. It is those kinds of individuals who belong to the 10%Club.

I hope you are inspired enough to join the club and create your own success in life.

If you analyse your core beliefs and values you will find your integrity and begin to live your life on purpose.

I remember as a young girl at school I decided that I wanted to make a difference in the world and leave a legacy. I wasn't sure how I was going to do that, but I did know that I had a burning passion to achieve more. Not for greed, purely for the sake of understanding what I need to know to make a difference for others, especially those with less then me.

If you have that burning desire in your heart to help others, please begin with yourself. To be extra-ordinary learn what you don't know.

The habit of role – model – Day 5

So whom did you acknowledge as being extra-ordinary?

Do you know why you were asked to write such a list?

The reason we chose to ask you to do that was to ignite your memory and awaken what lies within you - the desire to take your life to the next level and help others to do the same.

Throughout this mini self coaching course I am encouraging you to build your self-development, to begin self-coaching and to raise your personal standards. FOCUS on your lifestyle that you really want. Begin to believe you have what you want. Begin to create your lifestyle now.

Let's raise standards.

Expand your boundaries and raise your standards. It's by raising those standards that you'll make a breakthrough to your chosen destination.

How would you rate yourself in the following 8 areas on a scale 1 - 10?
SCORE code   10   represents the highs, excellent, the best
                  1   represents the need to improve considerably

1   Health & Fitness
2   Home & family & friends
3   Career
4   Finances
5   Spirituality
6   Very personal area   (by this we mean a private issue)
7   Leisure and fun activities
8   Personal development (CPD)

THE CIRCLE OF LIFE – Day 6

I can now tell you more about that very popular tool for self-development and coaching *THE CIRCLE OF LIFE*. It's a pie chart that gives you an instant picture into what values you place on your current lifestyle.

It is intended to be part of your personal *'blue print' plan* that needs to happen if you really want to change your life in seven days.

In this general illustration of the Circle of Life, I've given you 8 sections.
Name each section from the list below:

Health & Fitness.   Home & family.   Career.   Finances.   Friends.

Very personal area.   Leisure and fun activities.   Personal development.

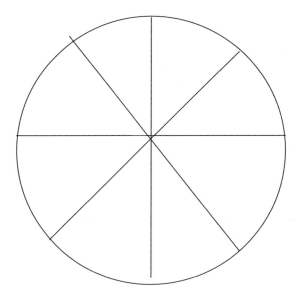

THE AIM of the *Circle of Life* exercise after completing the 8 sections results in a new outer circle. This new circumference identifies the level of *work and life balance* in your life. You will have in front of your eyes an accurate picture of what you believe your lifestyle to be today. It's a great tool.

The centre of the circle represents   0   = indicates the need to improve
                                                                  Considerably, least satisfaction.

The outer edge of the circle represents   10   = excellent, the best you can be,
                                                                  most satisfaction.

HOW TO CREATE A NEW OUTER CIRCLE

In turn think about the satisfaction level of your current lifestyle of each of the named sections I have given you. Then give it a score from 0 – 10. Draw a line across the section to mark a new outer edge within that particular section. You may like to colour in each section using different colours to aid visualisation of your lifestyle.

The completed drawing portrays what you think about and the value of balance you place on your life as it is today. Self worth!

How round in proportion to a circle is your pie chart?

Are you amazed at the results of this task? What do you think now?

Write any thoughts about the results of the exercise in your PPCA-Z journal.

You have just completed for yourself the *CIRCLE OF LIFE.*

It gave you a very fast and tangible indication of what you think right now.

Now just for variety have a go at this visualisation exercise.

EXERCISE

Please visualise some fresh flowers. Or, imagine a plant that has had its roots cut away from it.

Those fresh cut flowers or the rootless plant will continue for a while to live on. For how long, we don't know.

The same is true of our thoughts.

Our thoughts live on for a while just like the flowers or rootless plant, and give off the illusion of being just fine.

Gradually the flowers/plant's fragrance will cease and its lustre will fade, wither and eventually disappear altogether. That also applies to thoughts.

As we let our thoughts dissipate so too does our environment. We can become a victim of our environment.

Are you a positively inclined person, or are you a victim of your environment?

You do realise that you have choices. Do you utilise your options?

7 Days to a New You! – Day 7 pulling it all together for the future

This programme of self-coaching tools is just the tip of the ice-berg, so to speak. I've created it to help you to clear away the clutter in your life, to take control of your lifestyle and achieve a phenomenal transformation and get what you really want in life. It's a results orientated system that brings together dynamic tools that create a 'win win' outcome. The programme contributes to your well being and guides you along your personal journey of discovery and goal achievement. It's not all plain sailing, PaTrisha-Anne and all the Ambassadors of *Personal Performance Coaching A-Z* expect a commitment from their clients to gain the desired results. Are you ready to commit to your future? I encourage you to work through the programme and tap into the power that is dormant within you. That way anyone with such tenacity deserves to claim their dreams by going beyond the boundaries of your current lifestyle and to focus on your goals. Go get what you want.

1   **Clarify the goal.**

To take your lifestyle to the next level you need to know what you want. Once you know what you want, you'll need to ask yourself 'why?' you want it. The 'why' is the driver to get you to goal.

Think about what you want.
Write it down in your PPCA-Z journal . Be specific in the choice of words. Include a timescale of when you want it by, and if appropriate a financial budget. This is all part of a realistic action plan to get you what you really want.

2   **Plan.**

That's right draw up your plan. Take all of what you wrote down for number 1 – Clarify the goal and begin to put in more details.

Think about the overall strategy. Realise you can only do so much.

3   **Action.**

First off think about your personal needs and what you need to do to get them met. Then think about your action and what actions you'll do today to realise your expectations. Take the time to invest in yourself. Take action now and write your action plan in your PPCA-Z journal to keep the communication of your thoughts and your actions flowing.

All action needs self-discipline and a regular evaluation, so evaluate regularly, better still be so focused and check it all out daily. You may need to formulate creative solutions to unexpected challenges that might arise.

Have fun it's important, you come first. Get a net-work. Networking is great fun and you just don't know who you are going to meet. Celebrate all you achieve. Look outside the box and your comfort zone so that any outcomes that were not wanted can be turned into a lesson learned and then into a celebration. Take serious responsibility for yourself.

Create a workable daily plan and any follow up actions you need to take.

Keep your standards raised.

4   **Structure = that's the framework. The 6-Step Coaching Model.**

Without a solid framework you could run around in circles.
Use the a6-Step Coaching model as your working model.

Remind yourself constantly of your goals and stick to them, but fine-tune the goal posts on a daily basis. Look and listen for clues about this.
It may help to set up a diary system and plot actions that have to happen towards goal achievement with deadlines.

Visual reminders may help too. I find those little brightly coloured florescent stickers strategically placed help to remind me of my daily actions towards my goals. Even a knot tied in your handkerchief.

Don't ever feel sorry for yourself, get over the situation and move on.

The Unique 6-Step Coaching Model

This tool is used by coaches the world over. I created the tool back in the 1970's from the childhood poem;

> *'I Keep Six Honest Serving Men*
> *They taught me all I knew*
> *Their names are What and Why and When and How and Where and Who'*

> *by Rudyard Kipling.*

The technique is to use the concept to ask quality questions. That's how you'll get quality answers to use as the action plan towards goal achievement.

Clarification of **what** you want and **why** is part of the five 'w' strategies.

When quality questions are asked a clear understanding of what is desired falls automatically into place. Focus is enhanced and outcome more easily achieved.

There are no hard and fast rules about how often a 'w' question is asked and in what order.

You can ask yourself '**what** do I want?', or '**what** do I really want?'

You'd move on to perhaps a **why** question. So, '**why** do I want X?'

Next could come a **who** question. '**Who** will be involved with me getting the goal of X?', or '**who** am I really doing X for?'. Another question, '**Who** can help me achieve X?'

A **when** question is all about the commitment of time.

Where, could be questions about where you have to go to get training to achieve X or where will you be when X happens.

The five **w** open questions automatically formulate the 'how-to' achieve the goal.

Finally define who you are. If you haven't done so yet write a list about yourself in your PPCA-Z journal.

Be certain that you know who you are and what you really want in your life. Make an agreement with yourself never to put up with, to tolerate anything this doesn't fit into your _new you_ lifestyle.

7 Days to a New You! is easy when you know how.

And this book is part of your learning experience to know how to achieve what you want in life.

You can attract anything you want in life. The cosmic ordering system allows that to happen. To place your order with the cosmic your values, your characteristics and habits need to be fine tuned to allow prosperity and abundance to come into your life.

Please take the time to build up your PPCA-Z journal. Give it a go. If you are serious about changing your life and creating a new you, then this book will most definitely help you to being your journey.

If you'd like to, then why don't you write to me via the web site and let me know how you are getting on; www.lifecoachschoolinternational.co.uk I'd like to read your about your progress and I'll send you regular updates about my worldwide self development, business WorkLifeBalance seminars which you might want to attend with your family, friends and work colleagues, updates on my new books, CD releases and our new LCSi Radio programmes.

The idea and objective of this book

The idea behind this book is to share with you the idea that regardless of who you are, or what you do and where you live and work anything is possible if you put your mind to it.

It is for that reason I have put together this collection of personal stories written by a handful of some the graduated students of LCSi-LifeCoach School international.

It's a testimony to faith and belief in the core system of positive expert coaching.

It is said that knowledge is power. Each and every one of the ambassadors is living proof that the application of the 6-Step Coaching Model enhances personal performance.

Each story is unique and tells the journey of pain and triumph. As you read their words you may recognise their journey. Perhaps it's similar to what you have experienced or are currently going through.

Personal Performance Coaching A-Z takes the reader through the process of self-coaching towards his or her own goal using your own potential.

LCSi and the contributors of this self-coaching resource encourage you to enjoy the words crafted within the pages and explore self motivation and to find enhancement towards your own - Personal Performance Coaching A-Z.

What is Personal Performance Coaching?

Personal performance coaching is about your lifestyle and setting a change in motion. It's about the continuum of application and knowing how to deliver your best.

It's also about knowing how to fine tune personal skills towards achieving any desired personal goals.

However, with all the good will in the world and self-help books, (just like this one), and courses on self-development and the 'how to' courses to achieve the desired results; nothing will happen unless consistent personal effort is applied on a daily basis towards the goal.

It doesn't matter what that goal is. Be it to be the perfect parent, a role model, a teacher, a great employee or boss even dreams and aspirations of becoming a mega star, learning to drive or wanting to be a millionaire. The trick is to apply realistic daily action towards that goal.

So how convinced are you that you can change your lifestyle?

Well, the good news is you can, and you do that by adopting a new top level behaviour. Swiftly and permanently.

Top level behaviour requires a crystal clear vision of the future, be that future short term, or medium or long term. It also requires the skills of personal leadership and being able to take one-self to where you truly wish to go.

You can do this in as little as 60 seconds. Single minded focus on the desired goal area in hand leads to success and you will never feel lost or frustrated ever again.

It is this ability to concentrate on the goal and knowing why you want that goal that will spur you on to plot a plan of action that will produce the desired results. Your dedicated focus allows clarity of vision to gently but firmly develop your strength within the desired goal area. It's known as congruence.

Having a vision is the future; it allows you to think for the long term. So your perspective is captured and your future is guaranteed.

Furthermore integrity to yourself helps formulate the whole process.

Wow, how exciting is that to know you can be master of your own destiny.

The beginning of any journey begins with that first step.

Awareness of what you truly desire is the beginning of that process.

This book has been written to offer you the beginnings of that process.

Enjoy your journey.

Rules of the game for Personal Performance

Here is a list of Seven rules to help you take your life to the next level while you follow t he programme *7 Days to a New You!*

1. **Focus** on your life and enjoy your lifestyle while you help others to enjoy theirs. It's fun. Go on give it a go.

2. Turn your dreams into reality by daily application of your **blue-print** goal action plan.

3. Understand who, you really are and that with each day you age be thankful you have a little more wisdom to move forward in a positive way. Practice an **attitude of gratitude** policy.

4. Know your strengths and your weaknesses. Work diligently on your health system, your wealth system and your love of mankind. **Do it daily**.

5. **Step into your power** and enjoy your life from this moment on. Remember, life is not a rehearsal!

6. You can enjoy your life and plan to leave a legacy that will bring joy to the one's you leave it too. **Share** and reap the benefits.

7. Finally look forward to your life as you live it each day and advance into the future. Don't be afraid of anything. Make it your business to **find out** what you don't know.

The A – Z of Personal Performance Coaching

A

Achievement [celebration of achievement]

Access [recognising opportunity]

self Authority [knowledge]

Attitude [PMA]

B

Behaviour [Daily application towards goal]

Benefit [Sharing with others]

Building [Step-by-step]

C

Can't [Oh yes you can if you drop the 't']

Can [You know that you can with application]

Culminate [The sum total]

Celebrate [✓]

E

Effort [You are master of your own destiny]

Energy [Practice Incredible Self Care]

Enthusiasm [✓]

F

Faith [Find a role model to deepen your faith in yourself]

Forge ahead [Choose realistic steps]

Fulfill [✓]

G

Generate [Daily application will generate a daily outcome]

Goal [Use the 6-Step Coaching Model to discover your true goal in life]

Grace [Charity]

H

Heal [Visit your comfort zone when you need to rest and heal]

Health [Practice Incredible Self Care]

Higher self [Expand your consciousness]

I

Inner [Turn your inner thoughts into reality]

Insight [Work with a coach for insight]

Inspire [Lead by example]

Intuition [✓]

J

Joker [Laugh and learn]

Journey [Spiritual Journey Cosmic Coaching]

Jubilation [✓]

K

Knowledge

L

Laughter [Laugh every day and share your joy]

Life [You were born to live]

Lift [Elevate your lifestyle – *today*]

Love [✓]

M

Mental [PMA - positive mental attitude]

Mine [Dig deep into the *'minefield'* of your life]

Myself [✓]

N

Negative [Negative Mental Attitude]

No [Know the difference between Yes and No]

O

Open [Open your mind to opportunity]

Opinion [Keep yours to yourself]

Opportunity [✓]

P

Positive [Keep a positive mental attitude]

Power [✓]

Q

Quality [Expect quality]

Questions [✓]

R

Right [Choose you own direction]

Realistic [Keep your goals real]

Reality [✓]

S

Salvation [LCSi helps others]

Strength [develop yours]

T

Team effort [Share within your community]

Trial [Test out new ideas]

Together [✓]

EPILOGUE

This book, *Personal Performance Coaching A-Z* is a comprehensive resource for those individuals who search for personal empowerment as well as for those who are hungry for success. The book can be used as a contribution toward your own self-development journey. It is packed with stories of pain and triumph. The book also includes the dynamic mini-course;

'7 Days to a New You'.

A mini course of the whole version of the *90 Days Cosmic Ordering* programme.

Personal Performance Coaching A-Z can be used (in conjunction with *LifeCoaching A-Z*) by Life Coaches as an aid to effective coaching. Also, to gain an insight into, and, to understand how to begin a successful coaching practice.

The process of effective Life Coaching is very powerful. It encourages individuals to step out of their box away from their comfort zone and to take responsibility for their own actions which are the direct results of their thoughts. Infinite Intelligence is the source of mind power.

Life Coaches can help individuals and business owners to excel, as well as entrepreneurs and multi-national corporations achieve their business goals. All the contributors in this book hope they have helped you to understand the coaching process, to have made it clear for you, and to offer you direction and encouragement in self-responsibility for daily action towards your goal.

The Ambassadors of personal performance coaching are; Joy Allen, Halley Brentt, Claire Conroy, John Ellis, Ann Fieldhouse, Margaret Haffenden, Rose Hebbron, Marusja Harasymiw, Francelyn Lewis, Anthony Matthews, Simran Ranu, and PaTrisha-Anne Todd who all believe, *Coaching Leads To Success*.

LCSi
LifeCoach School international
LONDON Coaching School institute
LifeCoaching SCOTLAND institute
LifeCoaching School IRELAND

INVITATION

If you seriously want to change your life you can.

Join PaTrisha-Anne
on the 90 Days Cosmic Ordering Programme
and collect in 90 Days.

90 Days Cosmic Ordering Programme and collect in 90 Days.

Create your own destiny and Circle of Life having fun doing it.

Recognise your point of power and how to raise your standards.

Learn how to build your motivation and keep track every day on what you want.

You'll become a people magnet and a people millionaire a true power source for your own lifestyle.

Learn how to become financially free and live a healthy lifestyle.

Practice *Incredible Self Care*

On the 90 Days programme you can have more health, more wealth, better relationships and be happy, smile and experience joy, bliss, personal growth and business profit. It's guaranteed!

About LCSi - LifeCoach School international

LCSi was created at the turn of the century – the new millennium, a spin-off from the personal development services I had started in the 1980's. LCSI is an entity a one-stop educational resource providing quality professional sought after LifeCoach training and Personal and Corporate Performance programmes.

The training programmes significantly contribute to today's competitive self-development coaching world and students from all walks of life and corners of the world take on our training to gain a qualification and the knowledge to start and grow their own Life Coaching business.

LCSi – LifeCoach School international is a leading provider of effective Personal Performance and Corporate training, recognised the world over.

Work Life Balance programmes for small, medium enterprises to global consortiums seek LCSi trained coaches for their performance solutions. We can work with you on your performance coaching programme worldwide.

What LCSi can offer you:

The LCSi training products and services are consistently reviewed and updated to meet the ever demanding standards set by various bodies of coaching, though at the time of writing in 2006 there is no government or other official body that regulates LifeCoaching and named variations i.e. NLP, corporate, spiritual...

Accreditation for the Life Coach

Accreditation is important, as it sets a standard but as you now aware, Life Coach accreditation is not currently a government directive but an in-house process set up by private companies. Any training academy or organisation can pay an annual fee for the right to submit their training materials to that 'body' and to advertise that they are accredited by that association or federation.

LCSi-LifeCoach School international supports the self regulation process and remains an independent training provider and strives to go beyond any standards that may be set by other Life Coach training schools and organisations. We can and do meet coaching standards set and go beyond to excellence. The Ambassadors of Personal Performance Coaching are testimony to LCSi training.

LCSi services

Offer a comprehensive range of personal development and business growth products, each designed to deliver long-term change, transition and desired results.

Consulting

PaTrisha-Anne personally works with organisations to evaluate and set in place in-house corporate coaching. She can draw upon the expertise of the LCSi Ambassadors worldwide to support and achieve strategic organisational results. She also offers, Personal Cosmic Energy Ordering & Wealth Creation coaching.

Life Coach Training e-Courses

Foundation level.

Certificate level a qualification to work one-to-one with coaching clients.

Diploma level is the next up-grade from the Certificate level allowing you to work with teams, small groups and within the corporate arena. You can specialise in NLP, Cosmic Energy Coaching or Wealth Creation Coaching.

All three levels are distance learning courses downloadable from the internet. Support telephone coach calls can be booked by appointment.

Optional live intensive practical coaching days are offered to students as a resource for further dynamic training.

The Master level coaching course is designed for you to work with very large groups and to offer executive coaching services to exclusive clients. This six days training is offered twice a year with PaTrisha-Anne. Optional 1:1 training.

Authorship

PaTrisha-Anne is available for writing projects on motivation and personal and professional development. Publications, newspapers, magazines, books and film, show and TV, film and radio scripts.

Key-note

PaTrisha-Anne, is an international speaker specialising in motivation and personal and professional development talks and seminars.

You can invite PaTrisha-Anne to speak at your next event, conference, convention and radio and television programmes.

Engagements have been worldwide from UK based groups, clubs and companies, to entrepreneurial women's groups in India, USA metaphysical educational establishments and to American presidential meetings in Texas,

For further information please contact;

info@lifecoachschoolinternational.co.uk

+44 (0)1202 389998

www.lcsi.co.uk   www.patrishaanne.com

Titles by PaTrisha Anne

Pepper Your Life With Dreams　　*The little book on LifeCoaching and Inspiration*
ISBN 0-9543262-0-2　　　　　　　　£4.99

LifeCoaching A – Z　　　　　　*The ultimate guide to becoming a Life Coach*
ISBN 0-9543262-1-0　　　　　　　　£14.99

Personal Performance coaching A-Z　　*7 Days to a New You!*
　　　　　　　　　　　　　　　　　The Ambassadors of Coaching
ISBN 0-9543262-2-9　　　　　　　　£12.99

You can order direct from quality book stores and LCSi
books@lifecoachschoolinternational.co.uk
01202 389998

Available in 2007

Think & Grow Rich A-Z　　　　*The Law of Attraction for financial freedom*

ISBN 0-9543262-5-3　　　　　　　　£14.99

Cosmic Ordering　　　　　　　*Spiritual Journey Soul Energy Coaching*
ISBN 0-9543262-3-7　　　　　　　　£12.99